SNAP SHOT™

Art director Roger Priddy
Editor Mary Ling
Designers David Gillingwater,
Sharon Grant

Photography by
Frank Greenaway, Neil Fletcher,
Jane Burton, Kim Taylor,
Stephen Oliver and Colin Keates

SNAPSHOT™
is an imprint of Covent Garden Books.
232 Madison Avenue,
New York, New York 10016

Copyright © 1994 Covent Garden
Books Ltd., London.
2 4 6 8 10 9 7 5 3 1

ISBN 1-56458-554-9

Color reproduction by Colourscan
Printed in Belgium by Proost

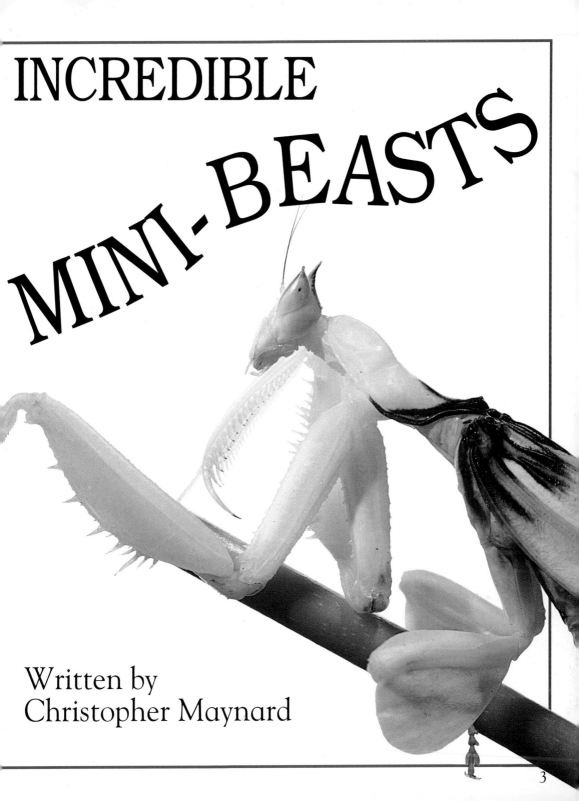

INCREDIBLE
MINI-BEASTS

Written by
Christopher Maynard

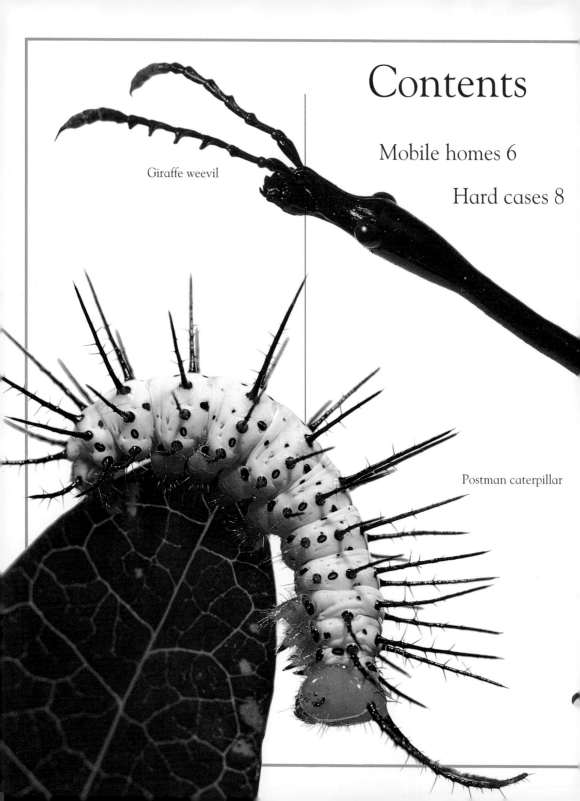

Contents

Giraffe weevil

Postman caterpillar

Mobile homes

Some animals are happy with just one address. Others have homes that are small enough to move anywhere they choose.

The home that grows!

Shell thickens and grows stronger.

Hermit crab

Great pond snail

Home addition
The great pond snail has a long, twisted shell on its back. As it grows, it builds a bigger shell. Only its head and foot peek out.

Adult caddis flies look a lot like moths.

Stuck at home

A caddis fly larva spins a tube of silk around its body. It sticks sand, pebbles, and bits of plants over this to hide itself.

Caddis larva

Wherever it goes ... home goes, too!

Caddis larvae use glue and silk to make cases.

Trading places

A hermit crab lives in borrowed shells. When it outgrows one shell, it moves to a new and bigger one - like this empty whelk shell.

Hard cases

There are more kinds of beetles than any other animal in the world. We know of about 300,000 species so far, compared to only 4,500 species of mammals.

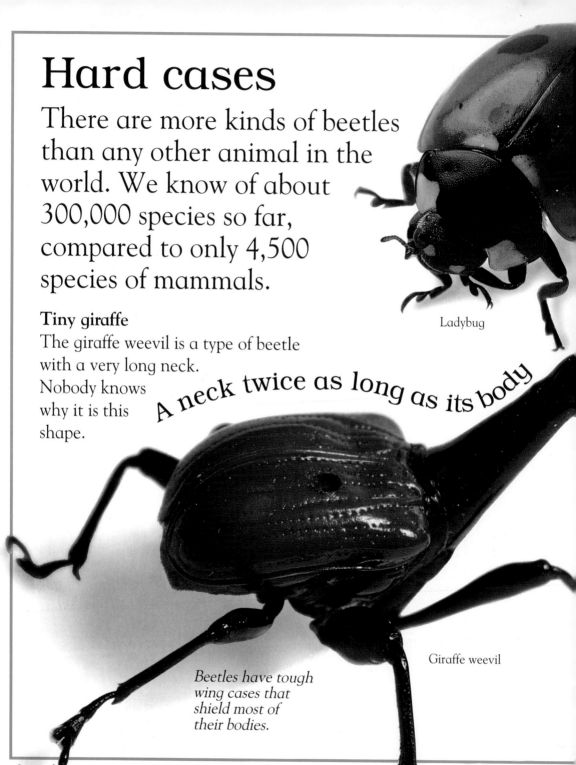

Ladybug

Tiny giraffe
The giraffe weevil is a type of beetle with a very long neck. Nobody knows why it is this shape.

A neck twice as long as its body

Giraffe weevil

Beetles have tough wing cases that shield most of their bodies.

Spot the spots

The ladybug is a bright red beetle speckled with black spots. These spots warn birds that ladybugs taste absolutely awful.

Powerful jaws for biting and chewing

Mouth on a pole

Many weevils' jaws are on the end of a long snout. This makes it easy for them to drill holes through wood and nuts.

Grabbing a bite to eat

Frog beetle

Frog march

Frog beetles have strong back legs that they use to leap away from danger – just like frogs. Once clear, they unfold their hind wings and fly away to safety.

Beetles use their hind legs to take off.

Munching machines

Caterpillars are eating machines.
A single one can polish off every leaf
on a bush during just a few days of
nonstop feasting.

They like spike!
This postman caterpillar has sharp,
poisonous spikes all along its back to
protect it from hungry birds.

Long
spikes

Gobbles thousand

Postman
caterpillar

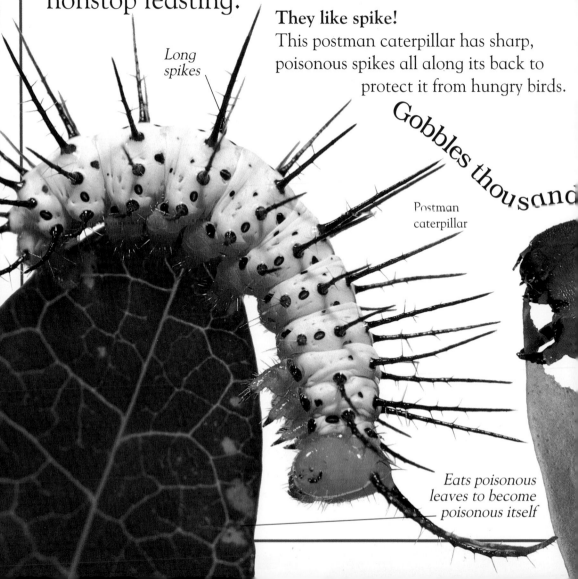

Eats poisonous
leaves to become
poisonous itself

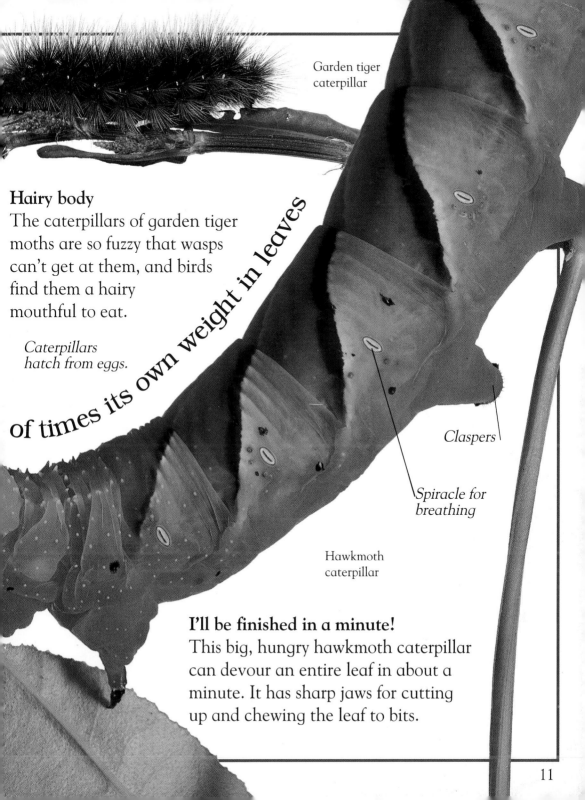

Garden tiger
caterpillar

Hairy body
The caterpillars of garden tiger
moths are so fuzzy that wasps
can't get at them, and birds
find them a hairy
mouthful to eat.

*Caterpillars
hatch from eggs.*

of times its own weight in leaves

Claspers

*Spiracle for
breathing*

Hawkmoth
caterpillar

I'll be finished in a minute!
This big, hungry hawkmoth caterpillar
can devour an entire leaf in about a
minute. It has sharp jaws for cutting
up and chewing the leaf to bits.

Butterflies and moths

Most butterflies are busy during the day, while moths fly around mainly at night. Aside from that, moths are often a drab brown, while butterflies have glorious colored wings.

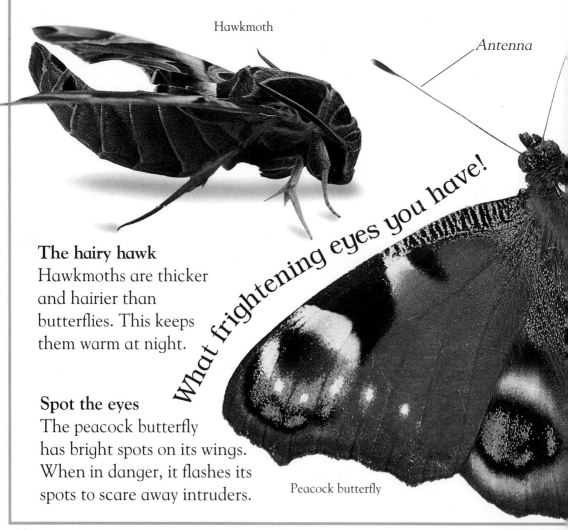

Hawkmoth

Antenna

What frightening eyes you have!

The hairy hawk
Hawkmoths are thicker and hairier than butterflies. This keeps them warm at night.

Spot the eyes
The peacock butterfly has bright spots on its wings. When in danger, it flashes its spots to scare away intruders.

Peacock butterfly

A lady's scent
Male moths can smell females with their antennae.

Sipping nectar
The bush moth has a long tubelike tongue for dipping into flowers and sucking out nectar.

What is making that smell?

Wing patterns are made up of thousands of tiny scales.

Bush moth

These pretty spots are not for decoration.

A butterfly sucks nectar through its straw-shaped 'proboscis.'

Seriously deadly

A hairy tarantula may be scary to look at, but watch out for its bite! It is deadly to birds and small animals, but only as bad as a bee sting to human beings.

Look out for a spider that's big and hairy!

Tarantula

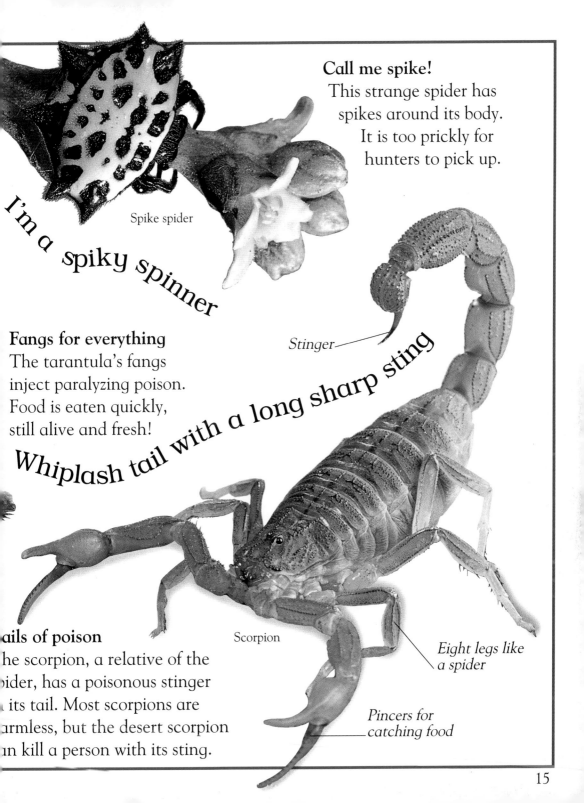

Spike spider

Call me spike!
This strange spider has spikes around its body. It is too prickly for hunters to pick up.

I'm a spiky spinner

Fangs for everything
The tarantula's fangs inject paralyzing poison. Food is eaten quickly, still alive and fresh!

Stinger

Whiplash tail with a long sharp sting

ails of poison
he scorpion, a relative of the ider, has a poisonous stinger its tail. Most scorpions are armless, but the desert scorpion n kill a person with its sting.

Scorpion

Eight legs like a spider

Pincers for catching food

Damsels and dragons

Most dragonflies are bigger than damselflies, although they look a lot alike. One difference that dragonflies hold their wings outspread wh damselflies fold their wings over their bodies.

Twenty to one
In flight, a dragonfly's wings beat about 20 times every second - so fast they are just a blur. They can fly 16 mph (25 km/h), making them very fast moving insects.

Dragonfly

Faster than a speeding bee?

Fly-catching legs
Their spike-covered legs hang beneath them and can snatch gnats, flies, and even wasps and bees in midair.

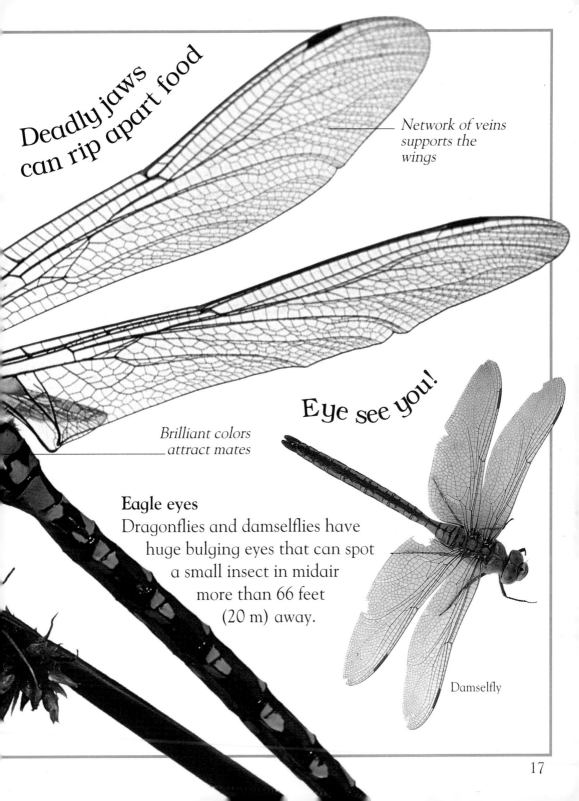

Deadly jaws can rip apart food

Network of veins supports the wings

Brilliant colors attract mates

Eye see you!

Eagle eyes
Dragonflies and damselflies have huge bulging eyes that can spot a small insect in midair more than 66 feet (20 m) away.

Damselfly

Lots of legs!

Most people think millipedes have 1,000 legs, and centipedes have 100. In truth, millipedes only have up to 750 legs, and centipedes from 30 to 354.

Legs move waves – so they don't get tangle

Nibble, nibble
Millipedes graze o algae or nibble on pla Some are even garden pests. They only come out at night to feed. By day, they hide in dark places.

Millipede

Long legged and built for speed

Centipedes have much longer legs than millipedes.

Seven times more
Compared to humans, most insects have an incredible number of legs. The common woodlouse, for example, has 14 legs in all.

Antenna

Woodlouse

Death by poison
Centipedes hunt snails, worms, and other insects, injecting poison into prey with their terrible fangs.

Beware the poison fang!

The sting thing

Bees and wasps have a needle-sharp stinger at the end of their tails. It delivers venom that can really hurt. Bees can only sting once before they die but wasps can sting many times.

Beware of the sting in the tail!

Wing

Stop signs
Wasps have bright yellow and black bands that warn other animals they are armed and dangerous and not very good to eat!

The honey bunch

When honeybees land on a flower they suck out sweet nectar with their tube-shaped mouths. Back at the hive, the nectar is turned into honey.

Bee

Bulging eyes

Wasp

The easy way to make honey

Recycled paper

Wasp nests are built from wood fiber that has been chewed up to make paper. A single egg is laid in each six-sided cell.

Powerful jaws are used for digging and cutting up food.

Growing larva

Bug eat bug

Insects that live by killing other insects need to be fast and strong. One of the best known hunters is the praying mantis.

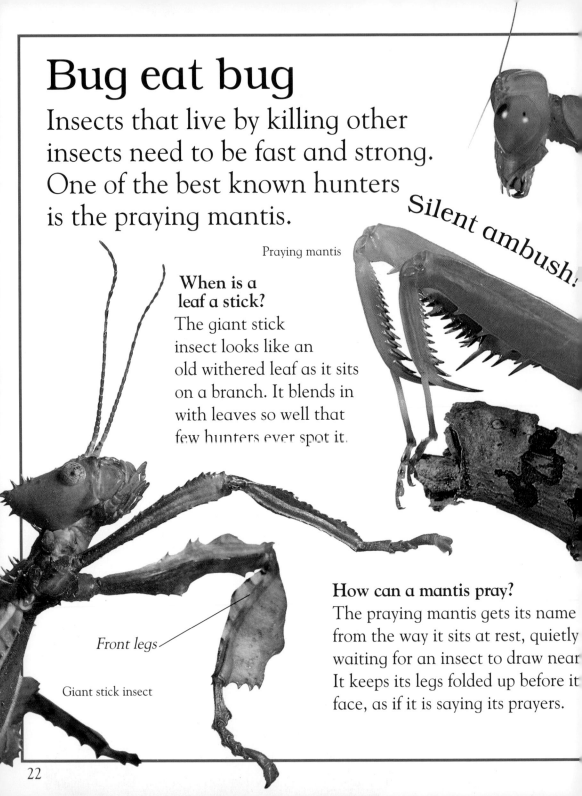

Praying mantis

Silent ambush!

When is a leaf a stick?

The giant stick insect looks like an old withered leaf as it sits on a branch. It blends in with leaves so well that few hunters ever spot it.

Front legs

Giant stick insect

How can a mantis pray?

The praying mantis gets its name from the way it sits at rest, quietly waiting for an insect to draw near. It keeps its legs folded up before it face, as if it is saying its prayers.

Just praying to be picked?

Orchid mantis

The leaf bites back!

Flower power
The deadly orchid
mantis hides among
orchids, pretending
to be a flower.

*Green body
helps hide it
among leaves.*

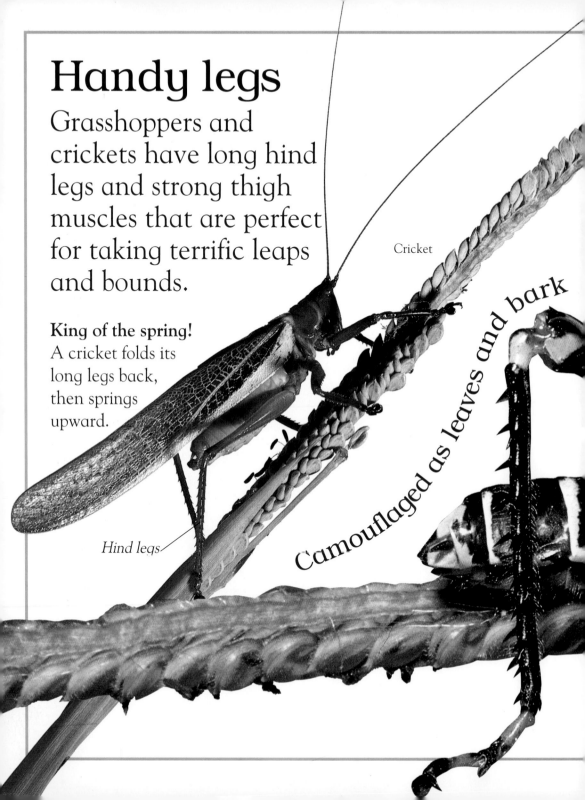

Handy legs

Grasshoppers and crickets have long hind legs and strong thigh muscles that are perfect for taking terrific leaps and bounds.

King of the spring!
A cricket folds its long legs back, then springs upward.

Cricket

Hind legs

Camouflaged as leaves and bark

Bush cricket

Long legs for great leaps

Flutter by
Once this bush cricket has launched into the air, its speckled wings fan out, and it flutters and glides away from danger.

A tasty hopper?
Like a wasp, this grasshopper has yellow and black stripes that say "yuk!" to the world, for this insect tastes awful.

Strong jaws chomp up leaves and grass

Treehopper

Old folks at home

Cockroaches have made their home on Earth for more than 320 million years, long enough to watch the dinosaurs roam the land and then disappear. During this time, they have hardly changed at all.

Antennae help find the way in the dark.

Cockroach

Home on the range
Cockroaches live almost anywhere. Several kinds have moved into human homes, where kitchens full of food crumbs are their favorite place.

Who's under the refrigerator?

Dark and damp

Some cockroaches love to live in caves, where it is dark and damp. Here they feed on almost anything: plants, fungi, dead animals, droppings.

Not afraid to stay in the dark

The flat body allows the cockroach to scurry into tiny crevices.

Young thing

Adults have a hard, shiny case to protect their wings. This cockroach is still too young to have grown any wings.

Young cockroach

Many mouths to feed

Insects feed in many ways. Some have strong jaws for tearing food to bits before they chew it up. Others have mouths best suited for piercing and sucking.

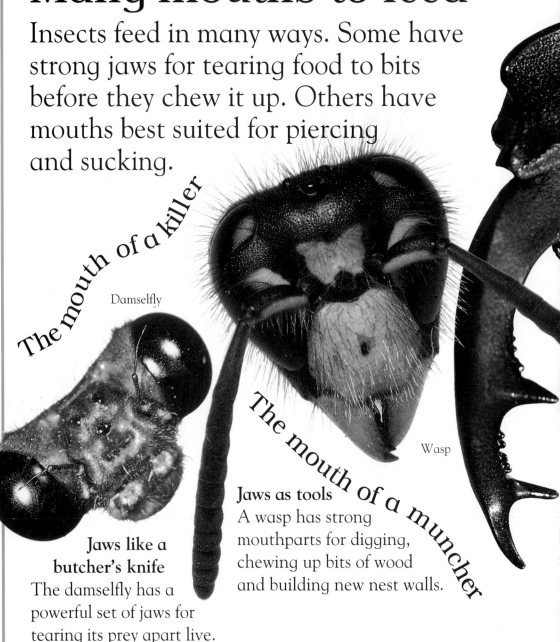

The mouth of a killer

Damselfly

The mouth of a muncher

Wasp

Jaws like a butcher's knife
The damselfly has a powerful set of jaws for tearing its prey apart live.

Jaws as tools
A wasp has strong mouthparts for digging, chewing up bits of wood and building new nest walls.

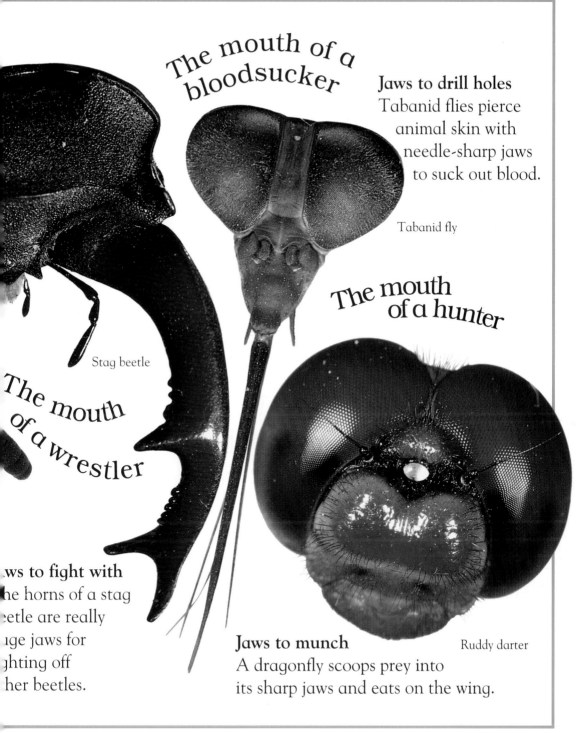

The mouth of a bloodsucker

Jaws to drill holes
Tabanid flies pierce
animal skin with
needle-sharp jaws
to suck out blood.

Tabanid fly

The mouth of a hunter

Stag beetle

The mouth of a wrestler

...ws to fight with
...he horns of a stag
...eetle are really
...ge jaws for
...ghting off
...her beetles.

Jaws to munch
A dragonfly scoops prey into
its sharp jaws and eats on the wing.

Ruddy darter

Index

Five fiendish questions

1. Which insect dress up in pebbles and san

2. How long does it take a caterpillar to eat a leaf?

(a) about 1 second
(b) about 1 minute
(c) about 1 hour
(d) several days
(e) caterpillars don't eat leaves

3. Which sense does male moth use to fin a female?

(a) sight (b) sound
(c) smell (d) taste
(e) touch

4. Will you die if a tarantula bites you?

5. How does a dragor catch its prey?

Answers on page 32

Are ladybugs always red with

black spots?

Answer on next page

Answers

From page 30 : 1. The caddis fly larva.
2. About one minute.
3. Smell
4. No, but the bite is as painful as a bee sting.
5. With its legs.

From page 31 : Not always. When they first hatch they are yellow in color. The red comes a few hours later.